Promises of an Afterlife: A Study of Near Death Experiences

By

ValkyrieKerry Kelly

Kelly Media © 2016 Reprinted 2018

Introduction

In New Testament theology it is stated that an everlasting afterlife is promised to those who live righteously according to the will of God;

For God so loved the world, that he gave his only Son, that whoever believes in him should not perish but have eternal life.

(John 3:16)

This complements the Old Testament belief in Sheol whereby the conscious self continues to exist after death. The scriptures of the Old Testament form part of all Mosaic religions; Christianity, Islam and Judaism. The New Testament, the section of the Bible utilised by Christians only, concerns itself with judgement. Jesus taught that judgement is based on the leading of a good life in which each person's aim should be to love others as him or herself, loving your neighbour as you love yourself. Judgement occurs after death whereby sinners are sent into purgatory, whilst the good rest in happiness with their Heavenly Father.

Buddhists have a slightly different approach, but again it reflects the idea of judgement. Individuals are reincarnated into a life according to their deeds in a previous life with the aim of achieving enlightenment to allow spiritual progression and release from an Earthly form. Buddhists, like Christians, believe in an ethereal realm in which other beings already reside, such as angels or in Buddhist terms; Demi-gods. There are references in the Bible to the seven heavens, particularly in the apocalyptic scripture 'The Revelations.' Similarly Buddhists recognise several realms outside of the Earthly including the realm of the hungry ghosts in which the souls of those attached to Earthly possession suffer in a state akin to purgatory.

These Mosaic and Buddhist belief structures both therefore propose that there is an afterlife and judgement is experienced after death with consequences to those dead for their actions on Earth, further both belief systems recognise pre-existing spiritual bodies that remain within those ethereal realms.

This investigation will examine, through case studies of modern day Near Death experients, in light of religious belief, the common factors found in experience and understanding of the afterlife.

The religious beliefs outlined above compare favourably to Dr P.M.H Atwater's current studies of Near Death Experiences. For example Atwater notes that 'One of the common aspects' is a Life review in which the experient perceives their entire life and experiences their positive and negative behaviours understanding the impact of the latter on others. This is a form of judgement and understanding erroneous behaviour and the impact on others through empathic examination and reflection.

The term Near Death Experience depicts the audio-visual effects envisaged by patients between loss of life and resuscitation. As such research into this area is phenomenological and provides qualitative data based upon personal recall and description. The data can be quantified by comparing common elements occurring across individual testimonies. The purpose of this investigation is to demonstrate that there are similarities across NDE case studies that support the key Mosaic and Buddhist ideas of; The Soul, An Afterlife, Judgement, Divine entities and Purgatory. It will be further demonstrated that these similarities range not only across these cases but support further the findings of previous similar studies. The Literary Review will allow some discussion of the findings of previous studies which support common features of the NDE and in doing so suggest validity of the experience.

The second part of the study concerns cross referencing the list of recurring factors with Buddhist and Christian theories of the passage to death and the first stage of the afterlife using depictions given in The Bible and in The Tripitaka focusing on primary sources as opposed to analytical secondary sources that may not be objective. The texts will be read and passages relating to the afterlife highlighted, analysed and key elements listed and compared. These will then be cross referenced with the recurring factors in NDEs to identify similarities. The findings will be summarised and discussed to provide an insight into the possible immediate experience of the conscious following death.

Literary Review

The purpose of this literary review is to identify how research to date in NDEs provide insight into life after death thus supporting evidence for the ongoing existence of the consciousness outside of the body. David Fontana (2005) explains that with modern medical technology patients can be resuscitated after death, even after brain death, stating that a period of oblivion in the gap between physical death and resuscitation would do nothing to support the notion of an afterlife or the existence of a soul or consciousness. However testimonies from patients offer no support of a period of oblivion. Instead they indicate that their senses remained not only acute, but heightened after death and such patients were able to recount events between death and resuscitation. This

Fontana believes, is promising for those who consider survival is a possibility.

The NDE is not a new phenomenon. In the 4th century BCE Plato told of the experience of a soldier called Er who apparently died in battle, but was revived on the funeral pyre. Er claims to have experienced his soul leaving his body and reuniting in a strange country where each comrade was allowed to choose his next life and once chosen acquired amnesia. This gives some support to the Buddhist notion of reincarnation as Buddhists and indeed Hindhus both believe in reincarnation. The story of Er supports not only the notion of reincarnation, but also the Buddhist idea of Karma; that the state of the next life will be based on actions in this one;

For he said that it was a sight worth seeing to observe how the several souls selected their lives. He said it was a strange, pitful, and ridiculous spectacle, as the choice was determined for the most part by the habits of their former lives.

(Chou (ed) 2003

http://www.wisdomportal.com/Technology/Plato-MythOfEr.html)

Fontana explains that a modern case akin to the case described by Plato was experienced by one Dr Wiltse in 1899 after enduring 30 minutes respiratory failure due to typhoid. Dr Wiltse describes being separated from his body as a blue hued soul. He was then lifted onto a road with a barrier, but told by other beings to return to Earth as his Earthly work was not yet complete. He was halted by a small black cloud and as soon as it touched his head he found himself returned to his body.

Both stories, over 2000 years apart, demonstrate an ongoing consciousness and the transportation of that consciousness to another location. Dannion Brinkley

(Brinkley and Perry 1994) had a NDE after being struck by lightning. Brinkley found himself not only detached physically from his body, but also detached from all Earthly interests and engulfed by peace and tranquillity thereafter he found himself transported through a tunnel and was met by a being of light. This being persuaded him, like Dr Wiltse, to return to his body as he had more Earthly work to do. Brinkley (2014) describes how the experience positively affected him;

Truly, my life and spirituality have come full circle......... Life is the greatest and most precious gift we could ever be given; I urge you not to take it for granted for a single moment.

(http://www.dannion.com/dannion-brinkley-near-death-experience/)

Fontana reports that people's experience of being sent back to their body's to complete an Earthly work is a common occurrence in reported NDEs as is references to meeting with either deceased relatives or beings of light. In terms of Religious ideology Jesus returned to Earth following crucifixion to give the apostles the gift of the Holy Spirit. This enabled the apostles to carry the teachings of Jesus across new lands. Sometimes these missions to return to Earth are optional and at other times pre-determined by the other being, for example the experient Eadie (1995) states that he knew that he had to come back as he was compelled by a mission of Earthly work.

One of the earliest medics to carry out research into the field of NDEs was Dr Martin Sabom (1982) whose position as a cardiologist working in resuscitation gave him a wide range of case studies but was concerned about the fine line between clinical death and near death so for his studies he opted to examine the testimonies of those whose death would result from trauma that could be expected to result in irreversible biological death. Sabom contacted all such patients, except those suffering psychiatric illness, from two Florida hospitals asking if they had an NDE and if they were willing to discuss it.

Sabom interviewed 78 patients of which 34 stated they had a NDE. Interestingly he noted that there were no recognisable differences in the NDEs of those of a religious background and those without indicating that the NDE was not a vision born from social or cultural conditioning. Sabom had expected some degree of contrast between the cases which would reduce the experience to medical visions, however this was not to be the case. All of the 34 patients reported an awareness that death had occurred. They were further aware and conscious of a physical separation from their bodies.

In Sabom's study 54% reported being transported to another location and a sense of paradise within that location. 28% of cases stated that they had met with a bright light and 48% claimed to have met with other beings, whilst 23% reported a void or tunnel as in the case of Brinkley. All patients reported being aware of returning to their bodies, and this was often reported to be against their wishes as in Eadie's case. Following the NDE 77% of patients interviewed reported a greater belief in an afterlife with no correlation to a pre-existing faith indicating that the NDE itself induced a belief or stronger belief in an afterlife.

Kenneth Ring (1984) examined the effects and aftermath of the NDE carrying out in depth interviews with 111 experients and identified similar and compatible after effects across all interviewees. He noted that all fear of death had been removed and that goals and values redirected towards love and compassion and the development of spiritual values without the dogmatism of organised religion. He also noted that some of his cases developed psychic intuition after the experience. Ankerberg and Weldon (2004) having examined Ring's research state that, 'Ring views psychic development as a natural outgrowth of the NDE' (http://www.jashow.org/wiki/index.php/Life_After_Death_-_Part_4).

Ring then directed his attentions to cases whereby the patients had been born blind. He wanted to know if their NDEs allowed visual sensory experience to demonstrate that the surviving consciousness of the experient existed outside of the confines of the physical body. Ring and Cooper (1991) worked alongside 11 American Blind Associations and identified 21 suitable candidates who were blind and had a NDE.

Of the 10 candidates born blind he found that 5 experienced sight in their NDE. The other 5 were unsure as to whether they had sight or not. 10 of the total sample reported having seen their own bodies and it was found that the experiences of the tunnel, the feeling of peace, the void, the bright light, a life review and meeting with other beings were experienced the same as those who had sight. Two experients were able to describe the brilliant colours of the paradise of the afterlife. The blind experients reported that the experience was unlike a dream and Ring's earlier study found that the poor sighted experienced significant improvement in vision during their NDE.

Morse and Perry (1990) carried out a study of NDEs in 12 young children, NDEs were not directly discussed or raised to prevent manipulation of recollection the children were asked two questions;

Do you remember being unconscious? And what do you think happens when we die? 8 of the 12 reported leaving their bodies and travelling in a manner comparative to the testimonies of adults; as a consciousness free from the body. Morse ran a control group of medicated child patients who were sick and under the influence of drugs to confirm that the NDEs were not drug induced hallucinations and found that not one of the 121 children in the control group experienced an NDE.

This indicates that the experiences were not triggered by pharmaceuticals. Ten years after conducting his research Morse carried out follow up interviews with the subjects and found them to have humbling maturity and wisdom just as the adult experients redirected their lives towards love and compassion. The philosopher Schopenhauer was one of the earliest western academics to study Buddhism and he concluded that moral goodness come from 'Unselfish compassion for others' (Sprigge T L S 1995 pg.144)

The existing literature demonstrates that the common elements of the NDE include the presuppositions of Buddhist and Mosaic texts; that there exists a soul, that there is an afterlife, that a form of judgement occurs and that beings exist within that afterlife. Other common elements include; the idea of a tunnel, a bright light and the existence of other beings. The purpose of this study is to examine four case studies in detail to identify these elements as a common theme within those case studies and in the context of Mosaic and Eastern beliefs and further that they support the findings of Morse and Perry, Sabom and Ring.

Results

The first two sources selected as case studies come from; *Transformed by the Light* (Morse with Perry 1992) and *Light After Death* (Wilson 1997) Morse cites the experience of Barbara's sister told to Barbara during her Fourteen-year battle with leukaemia. Barbara herself is not an experient, but her sister disclosed details of an NDE which occurred during surgery. Barbara concedes that the experience did take place at a moment when her sister almost died. Barbara explains that she could tell through non-verbal communication that her sister was sincere in her account. The experient in this case describes feeling conscious of being drawn upwards whilst on the operating table. This movement started slowly but accelerated until she found herself in a black tunnel.

At the event horizon was a light which gained intensity with her proximity. The light was deemed beautiful and indescribable. As she neared the light her movement decelerated until the light was engulfing her. The light triggered emotions of love, joy and calm. She recalled wanting to remain in the light forever. This moment of perfect serenity could be compared to Heaven. This was followed by a life review in which everything she had done flashed before her. The review was interrupted by a feeling of falling back through the tunnel into her own body. On reflection she felt that the light was Jesus and thereafter she had a different attitude towards her illness putting others at ease by assuring them that death was not the end.

The case of Howard Storm, a Professor from Cincinnati, is told from the first person (Wilson) in great detail after collapsing whilst touring Paris in

1985. Storm states that his first moment of awareness after death was standing from an external loci watching his own body and his wife breaking down. He tried to draw the attention of the attendants, but they failed to acknowledge him, however at this point he felt dissociated from his body and unwilling to return to it. Storm found that his senses were heightened and he knew it was neither a dream nor a hallucination by comparison to past experiences of these states.

Storm became aware of other beings calling to him and perceived their silhouettes which beckoned him into a mist. The beings were depicted as malignant leading him into a darkness in which they tormented him through physical discomfort and he felt full of hopelessness. Much like the hungry ghosts of Buddhism. Subsequently he prayed and during prayer the beings backed away until none were left, but he was left in bleakness until he called to Jesus to save him. At that point a light appeared in the darkness and expanded rapidly towards him until he was surrounded by it and realised that the light was a loving being, much like the light that engulfed Barbara's sister.

Storm felt that the light elevated him from the darkness through space until other lights joined them. The lights explained that they could adopt human form and were omnipresent and telepathic and able to feel our emotions. Storm describes feeling unworthy. He then experienced a life review in which the beings were not concerned with personal achievement, but with how he had interacted with others rejoicing at the moments of love and compassion. The life's review is shown as challenging but the therapy to assist came from the love of the others and whilst undergoing this experience he felt that the slate was being cleansed.

Storm was then told he had to return and shown that inanimate objects; religious objects mean nothing concluding that loving people and living with people is what's really important. Just as Jesus had taught in the New Testament.

Indeed during Storm's experience he reported engaging in discourse with Jesus and Angels and during this meeting he asked questions about the nature of the afterlife and existence. Laurence (2010) describes one such encounter;

The angels that Howard Storm saw while on the other side answered many questions that he posed. When he asked where creation came from they answered that there was never time, matter or space before God. God created universes which became proactive, and there are countless intelligent beings in the universe.

(http://www.examiner.com/article/predictions-from-jesus-given-to-howard-storm-after-he-died)

This report suggests that God is the source of the universe. A similar proposal is made in Lao Tzu's Tao Te Ching a scripture from an Eastern philosopher in which God is seen as the eternal source. Although not a Buddhist text the Tao Te Ching is held in Buddhist monasteries.

George Rodonia's experience is told in the first person at http://www.near-death.com/experiences/evidence10.html and is taken from Berman's (1998) *The Journey Home*. Rodonia's case is exceptional in that he was deemed dead for three days and his experience is detailed and prolonged. Following the experience Rodonia became a Minister.

Rodonia found himself surrounded by darkness and only attracted the light through positive thinking. The light's brilliance is depicted as painful initially, but becomes warm and comforting and Rodonia states that he underwent a life review. Through the light he gained an understanding of the unity of the universe with all of the 'molecules' coming together in perfect symmetry in 'timeless unity.' He shows detachment from feelings experienced in his mortal life and describes an almost omnipotent ability to experience and understand everything Earthly when the mind is open to it by choosing to experience points in time and space. During his encounters he states that he attempted to communicate with past figures, but was unable to do so although some sensed his presence.

On resuscitation Rodonia felt changed through his new belief that God is more than the light, he is everything in light and darkness and that organised religion fails to define God because God is indescribable and he now believes in God of the

Universe. Rodonia (2013) describes his changed perceptions of God as follows;

All I can say is that I now believe in the God of the universe. Unlike many other people, however, I have never called God the light, because God is beyond our comprehension. God, I believe, is even more than the light, because God is also darkness. God is everything that exists, everything

(http://www.near-death.com/experiences/evidence10.html)

The final case comes from the research site http://www.nderf.org/NDERF/NDE_Experiences/frank_g_fde.htm and is attributed to Frank G (2013) who experienced his NDE following a rock climbing accident in Britain. Frank's immediate feeling was that time had stood still and he was engulfed in darkness, but felt content and happy. This feeling preceded access to universal knowledge, much like

Rodonia's, and a connection with everything and that the connection gave him a sense of security and warmth akin to being loved and safe in the maternal womb, floating in real love, not the mortal equivalent.

During his experience Frank describes a floating sensation whilst surrounded by bouncing light balls and the compassion and love of all the people he had known. Frank then perceived beautiful natural scenery and other beings, but in amongst these positive experiences there was a ball of dark light with grasping hands that repelled Frank finally a 'tidal wave' came over him and everything 'vanished' as he came back to life.

The Bible and *The Tripitaka* do not describe the experiences of individual's close to death, but reflect the teachings of spiritual masters on the nature of the afterlife. Both texts are extremely expansive and subsequently only a handful of teachings will be discussed for the purpose of this study focusing on the afterlife. The most prevalent point Jesus makes throughout his sayings and parables is that Humans should love God and each other unconditionally and that, as in the parable of the prodigal son, there is always a chance for the redemption of sinners as God loves those who return to him. There is, according to the New Testament, an afterlife in which individuals are judged by God and Jesus can be called upon as an advocate.

I tell you, on the day of judgment people will give account for every careless word they speak,

(Matthew 12:36)

For those who are unable to repent purgatory is described; Then He will also say to those on His left, 'Depart from Me, accursed ones, into the eternal fire which has been prepared for the devil and his angels'

(Matthew 25:41)

Those who act in goodness have a special place in the afterlife;

In my Father's house are many rooms. If it were not so, would I have told you that I go to prepare a place for you?

(John 14:2)

God is depicted as the light that takes away the darkness;

This is the message we have heard from him and proclaim to you, that God is light, and in him is no darkness at all.

(John 1:5)

In summary the New Testament tells readers that there is an afterlife in which the individual will be judged and then directed to Heaven or Purgatory following judgement. Purgatory is defined as the darkness, a Hell like dimension, whereas God is the light.

The implications of altruistic behaviour leading to a positive afterlife experience also appears in the Buddhist text The Tripitaka;

Not even death can wipe out our good deeds

(Smolowe ed, 2013 http://www.greatthoughtstreasury.com/author/tripitaka-or-tipitaka?page=4)

In Buddhism samsara relates to purgatory, or hell depending upon personal interpretation, where ongoing suffering is inevitable. Nirvana is reached through compassion and detachment which led to enlightenment. Nirvana is the realm of heaven or escape from suffering.

Souls are trapped in an endless cycle of rebirth as they grasp for material gain and fail to practice compassionate detachment which would lead to enlightenment and Nirvana. Judgement exists in a form called karma in which past deeds result in present consequences and good deeds are rewarded whereas malignant deeds result in further suffering for the perpetrator. The suffering continues to allow personal growth. Perhaps this is why some experients are returned to their mortal body to complete their work or learning curve in that lifetime.

Hungry ghosts are souls reborn to suffer from their own vices as O' Brian (2014) writes

Beings are reborn as hungry ghosts because of their greed, envy and jealousy.

(http://buddhism.about.com/od/buddhismglossaryh/g/hungryghostdef.htm) just as Catholics recognise a state of judgement or purgatory where souls must be purified of their sins. These two descriptions may be comparable to the darkness endured by Rodonia. Slick (2014) describes the process of purification demonstrating the similarity to the Buddhist realm of the Hungry Ghosts whereby the soul suffers in accordance with its Earthly vices;

According to Roman Catholic Doctrine, though a person may be in a state of grace, he may not enter heaven until he is purified from sins that were not dealt with on earth. Baptism remits sins committed up to that point, but prayers, indulgences, penance, absolution, and the Mass are means by which the sinner is able to expiate sins committed after baptism. If sins are not remitted, after death he must suffer the flames of purification until he is sufficiently cleansed and pure so as to enter into the presence of God.

(http://carm.org/purgatory)

Buddha deemed belief in God unnecessary to lead a good life and escape the cycle of rebirth, however light is associated with positive deeds and living in the light projected as the ideal state. Pym (2011) believes that there is an agreement between Christians and Buddhists through the ideas of light and love;

The Buddha tells us the story of Amitabha, the Buddha of Infinite Light, while the Christian Epistle of John states that, "God is Light, and in Him there is no darkness at all". The obvious philosophical (theological? buddhalogical?) question that arises is; "Can there be two Infinite Lights?" As the answer is obviously "No", then it becomes clear that the Apostle John and the writers of the Pure Land scriptures are talking about the same thing, though using slightly different language. The Christian scriptures also state that "God is Love", and I have yet to meet a Buddhist who does not believe in Love.

(http://www.buddhist-christian.org/articles/0704jp.html)

The purpose of the results section of this study is to identify and summarise the key elements of each NDE and further to identify such elements in the Christian and Buddhist faiths. The first preternatural experience of Barbara's sister is that of her conscious being displaced away from her body suggesting that part of the self continues to exist after death or alternatively that the body is vehicle to carry the soul or self through life.

This aspect of the self, the conscious, has other names to identify it such as soul and spirit or atman. The self in Buddhism is part of a greater whole which supports Rodonia's understanding of universal unification. The concern here however is with detachment of the conscious from the physical body and for all intents and purposes that part of the consciousness will be deemed as the self or soul.

Barbara's sister cites being consciously perceptive outside of her body. This is described as a slow elevation leaving the body behind whereby her soul continued to exist without the body and detached from it.

The next element of Barbara's experience as a soul is rapid movement away from her point of origin and leads to the third element of the experience; the black tunnel which then leads to an intense light of serenity and love. Barabara's sister associates the light with Jesus and describes undergoing a life review. In simple terms she depicts six key elements: Detachment from the body, movement to another location, a tunnel, the beautiful loving light, a life review and possibly Jesus, a spiritual figure.

Storm also describes the detachment from his body and explains further that his senses were heightened. Initially Storm does not experience the light, but a tormenting darkness and malignant beings. He experiences the light after submitting to Jesus. At this point the light appears and expands until it engulfs him and moves him, so in agreement with Barbara's sister Storm experiences; displacement from his body, movement and a spiritual being but adds heightened sense to the equation and a realm of bleakness and malignant beings.

Once engaged with the light a life review occurs as does interaction with other beings of light that can take human form and advanced telepathy in which the beings of light show that they are capable of experience empathy and emotion for all living beings. Storm is made to understand that love and compassion are the most important factors in mortal life, so to summarise the key elements of storms experience are; detachment from the body, movement, a bleak realm, beings; mystical, possibly once human and malignant, the engulfing light, telepathy and an understanding of the importance of love.

Rodonia, like Storm, experiences a realm of darkness following displacement from the body. After positive thinking Rodonia is engulfed by the light and reviews his life, but then his experience deviates from the two previous experiences in that he perceives the natural state of the universe, its unity and its timelessness and this part of the experience supports Buddhist doctrine that there is an oneness in the universe. In Christian terms the emphasis on loving one's neighbour as thyself perhaps hints at a unity of all creation and ethereal existence.

Rodonia found himself able to witness and gain knowledge of any point in time or space almost omnipotently. Rodonia was transformed by his experience realising that God is God of the universe and indescribable in human terms. To conclude, the elements of Rodonia's experience include; displacement of the conscious, movement, a realm of darkness, the light, a life review, the unified nature of the universe, the ability to gain universal experiential knowledge and a greater awareness of the nature of God.

The final case study, Frank's story, begins as with the other case studies with displacement from the body and an engulfing darkness. In this darkness Frank feels content and happy. He also feels the love described by the other experients as part of the light. Although Frank does not experience the light he is aware of light balls that are bouncing around him.

During his experience Frank feels a unity with everything and finds he has access to extensive knowledge which provides further comfort and access to the love of all who have known him. He then finds himself in a beautiful natural scene, but within this scene are unwelcome balls of darkness which hold what are deemed to be malignant beings. The elements of Frank's experience are; displacement from the body, darkness, love, light balls, scenery, access to knowledge and malignant darkness.

The results show that all experients were displaced from their bodies and all experienced movement or a change of scenery which is indicative of movement. Three of the experients went through a life review after being engulfed by a loving light. Three also experience a malignant darkness.

All four experients note an awareness of other beings either as the light, the universe or as light balls. Two cases find that they can access universal knowledge, but only one refers specifically to telepathy and experiential viewing whilst all four refer to the love of or a better understanding of spiritual beings associated with God or Jesus. The common elements of the NDE in these studies are; displacement of the soul, a light of love, life review, malignant darkness, access to knowledge, spiritual beings and unity.

The life review is perhaps the most significant factor when examining religious texts. This life review is akin to Christian judgement or Buddhist Karma in that one has to experience consequences for negative actions.

The NDEs above suggest that this judgement occurs through analysis of actions and understanding and empathising with those who they have interacted with and caused pain. Equally positive actions are highlighted and rewarded as suggested in the

Tripitaka. In Biblical terms a positive judgement opens the door to eternal life, where as in Buddhist terms a positive judgement results in a higher birth.

The realm of darkness could relate to the Christian depictions of purgatory and the light of serenity could be interpreted as heaven and being at one with God. Jesus certainly depicts God as the light that takes away the darkness and Buddhists find Nirvana through enlightenment. There is also a suggestion that God provides the unity of the universe and is a gateway to omnipotent knowledge.

Discussion

Before discussing the implications of this study some of the limitations of it must be considered. In terms of scientific research the data examined here would not be deemed scientifically relevant as only four studies were used. Technically the common elements could be considered quantitatively with displacement occurring 4/4 times, movement 4/4 times, the Light 3/4 times, other beings 4/4 times and unity and knowledge 2/4 times. However for quantitative data to be examined statistically a much greater number of cases would be required.

At present the NDE Research Foundation holds over 3000 reported cases of NDEs and allows the experient to describe the experience qualitatively and then to answer such questions as 'Did you encounter other beings?' to provide statistically comparable responses.

The drawback of the subjective reports in both this study and the archives of the NDERF is that the data collected is based on subjective experiences and relies on the honesty of the subject. Very little tangible evidence is available. The NDERF recognises that some experients' cases are backed up by medical data in terms of loss of life and the experient providing details of incidences during the experience that they could not otherwise have known. To counter this there is Carl Jung's (cited in Gross 1990) theory of a collective unconscious in which we all share universal knowledge beneath the subconscious and the notion that in these cases the individual may have greater access to this information, however Wilson notes that in certain cases the brain has been dead during the experience and yet the experient has reported an awareness of events during the time of the brain's inactivity implying that a consciousness does exist outside of the parameters of the mortal body.

The various limitations suggest that a far greater study of NDEs is required to produce significant results and that the subject's medical history should be examined as part of that process as well as reports from those in the vicinity during the experience. With this borne in mind this discussion will examine some of the implications made in this study.

The most significant implication is that there is a soul or consciousness which can be culturally defined as the Nous (Greek) or Atman (Hindu) which contains the true self that is the personality, experiences, knowledge and character of the individual. This is indicated by the feeling that the soul has moved apart from the body, which as stated above appears to only be a vehicle or mechanism for allowing experience of mortal life.

It is likely that during life this soul is connected to the brain as the brain is the bodily location for processing experiences and following the NDE subjects recalled their experiences using normal cognitive processes and communication. Perhaps there is some truth in the saying that the eyes are the windows to the soul. This implication provides a passageway to the afterlife as the soul must continue to exist somewhere.

The experients felt that they were being transported at speed to another location, towards the light. It is interesting now to note parallels in modern physics. Stephen Hawkings (2010) proposes that in space there are anomalies called wormholes that can transport objects from one place in the universe to another at great speed. He goes on to explain that these wormholes have been found in the fabric of our world but are only minute in size, however larger wormholes could safely exist in space.

To understand why this is significant we must briefly consider the nature of the form of other beings as proposed by the experients. The other beings are depicted as balls of light and light is both a particle and wave that can travel at speed and can be refracted whilst having the capability to enter and travel through the tiniest spaces. In physical terms if the soul was somewhat like a light particle it could easily travel through immediate or other wormholes at speed without being damaged and regardless of the size. It may be then that what we consider heaven is reached through wormholes as the spirit takes the form of light. This would also explain the Biblical description of Elijah being taken up in a chariot of fire and Jesus' ascension.

The NDEs described here differ from the urban legend of simply going towards the light due to the appearance of a realm of a malignant darkness comparable to purgatory. Two experients describe a fearful darkness and one goes as far to say that there were beings intentionally taunting him and causing him pain. This conforms to the Christian notion of the gnashing of teeth due to the sufferings experienced by sinners in the afterlife. Equally in Buddhism this could refer to the realm where Hungry Ghosts are trapped between the mortal and ethereal dimensions suffering due to past actions.

What is noteworthy is that faith in a positive power calls the light and repels the darkness. In New Testament theology Jesus explains that whether the individual must believe in the Holy Spirit, in other words man must believe in a positive force permeating the universe and reach to that force when in need; 'ask and it will be given' (Matthew 7:7). In Storm's experience he asks for assistance in the darkness and the light saves him complementing the teaching in Matthew.

Once engulfed by the light experients describe feeling loved and even suggest that the light is God or Jesus and as such provides the comfort required prior to the life review. The life review reflects the New Testament judgement and the individual has the harshest judge; the self. The judgement and suffering come from the heightened empathy and sensory awareness which allows the experient to feel the effects their actions have on others. This supports the Mosaic commandments and Jesus' teaching that people should love their neighbour and turn the other cheek on the negative actions of others (Matthew 5:39) loving unconditionally and compassionately just as Buddhists are taught compassion for all beings.

The light overcomes the darkness and repentance can occur after death when the Kingdom of Heaven is close at hand (Matthew 3:2) by believing just as Storm found himself believing and was subsequently saved. The process of judgement is advocated by beings of light as depicted in 'John' 2:1-11 with love and compassion and as well as a telepathic or empathic understanding of how our Earthly actions sadden or enrapture those beings.

Two of the experients found that they had access to universal knowledge and identified the universe and God as one unified whole whose nature could not be defined in words. In modern physics the term entanglement is used to explain how every part of the universe is connected on a molecular level and Carl Jung, who also experienced a Near Death Experience believed further in a collective unconscious or shared knowledge again indicating a universal connection.

This connection allows the experient to access and understand the universe as a whole both scientifically and socio-historically. The experients found God indescribable, a similar experience was attributed to St Thomas Aquinas who wrote some eight million words on theology but ceased to write after a religious experience because he felt he could not put God into words. On his death bed Aquinas explained (cited by Sanders, 2010)

I adjure you by the living almighty God, and by the faith you have in our order, and by charity that you strictly promise me you will never reveal in my lifetime what I tell you. Everything that I have written seems like straw to me compared to those things that I have seen and have been revealed to me.

(http://www.patheos.com/blogs/scriptorium/2010/12/thomas-aquinas-big-pile-of-straw/)

These experiences and the feeling of love and the positive reflections of love in the life review indicate that the purpose of living is to love.

In the words of Jesus;

Do to others as you would have them do to you

(Luke 6:31)

In the words of the Buddha;

Consider others as yourself

Dhammapada 10:1 (Borg ed 1997).

Conclusions

The subjective experiences used in this study certainly suggest that the conscious self is quite separate and can exist independently of the human body and can continue to exist after the demise of the body. This implies that the body is simply a vehicle for allowing the conscious to experience a mortal life.

The conscious self or soul detaches from the body at death and continues to have experiences. When attached to the mortal body it is likely that there is some connection between the soul and the brain as events from the NDE are recalled on resuscitation. The NDEs described here also indicate that after death the soul is transported elsewhere.

There are no indications as to where this other plane of existence is located, except that one experient travelled upwards from her body suggesting movement away from the Earth and its gravitational pull. Frank experienced a blackness and Barbara's sister a dark tunnel, neither of which were deemed a threat, again suggesting travel elsewhere.

In three cases an all engulfing light enveloped the experients and that light was deemed emotionally aware and had the conscious form of a spiritual being related to Jesus or to God. As such it seems that the spiritual self is quite separate from the body and another dimension exists after death. This dimension is deemed timeless.

Biblical and Karmic judgement occurs in the life review, a common feature of the NDE, and consists of reflecting upon positive and negative actions toward others in one's lifetime. The important message is that approval is given to those who can experience love towards other living beings. This supports Jesus' mantra of loving one's neighbour as you love yourself and the Buddhist idea that positive actions receive positive rewards.

The experients felt that throughout the life review they were supported by loved ones or spiritual beings who did not judge as such, but empathised in a loving environment. The judgement is almost one of self-judgement as the individual reflects upon the suffering they have caused others and the good that they have done.

Two experients developed a realisation that there exists a unity in the universe and God permeates through that unity and after death found that they had access to worldly knowledge and a better understanding of the nature of God and the universe, but this understanding cannot be put into words nor explained within an Earthly context. The love and contentment within the light could be defined as heaven or in Biblical terms My Father's House and the access to knowledge the Many Rooms described in the New Testament.

However, there is also the bleaker aspect of the unpleasant darkness which could be considered purgatory or in Buddhist terms the realm of the Hungry Ghosts. Escape from the darkness appears to depend upon faith and love and the message imparted by the experience that the love of other living beings is the greatest Earthly achievement.

The nature of purgatory is given in some detail with two references made to the darkness and one to the suffering and pain experienced in that darkness. The darkness itself appears to contain malevolent beings intent on causing misery to the experient and thrusting torture and mocking upon the. Frank does not actually enter the darkness but recognises that he is afraid of it whereas Storm suffers directly within the darkness and at the hands of spiteful beings.

Buddhist scripture refers to those trapped between realms as 'Hungry Ghosts' whose bad karma has forced them to step down from the mortal realm into a realm of suffering and desperation. The beings within this darkness could be deemed hungry ghosts or in Biblical terms demons or the fallen. The experience of Storm follows the Catholic ideology that souls can be prayed for and saved after death and in this instance it is Storm's prayers that call upon the light to release him.

The key elements of the four NDE cases and the two religious traditions discussed are that the soul can exist after the demise of the body and that there is another plane of existence in which judgement occurs.

References/Bibliography

Ankerberg J and Weldon J (2004) *Life After Death* http://www.jashow.org/wiki/index.php/Life_After_Death_-_Part_4

Atwater P.M.H (2004) http://www.near-death.com/experiences/research24.html

Bodhi B (ed) (2005) *In the Buddha's Words: An Anthology of Discourses from the Pali Canon* (Tripitaka) Wisdom Books, London

Borg M (ed) (1997) *Jesus and Buddha: The Parallel Sayings* Ulysses Press, California

Brinkley D and Perry P (1994) *Saved by the Light* Villard Books, UK

Brinkley D (2014) *Near Death Experiences* http://www.dannion.com/dannion-brinkley-near-death-experience/

Chou Y (2003) *Odysseus Chooses His Next Life* Plato's "Myth of Er" http://www.wisdomportal.com/Technology/Plato-MythOfEr.html

Eadie B and Taylor C (1995) *Embraced by the Light* Bantam Books, New York

Fontana D (2005) *Is there an Afterlife?* Maple Veil, Pasadena

Gross R (1990) *Psychology: The Science of Mind and Behaviour* Hodder and Stoughton, UK

Hawkings S (2010) *Wormhole Voyages* Discovery Channel

Laurence A (2010) *Predictions from Jesus given to Howard Storm after he "died."*

http://www.examiner.com/article/predictions-from-jesus-given-to-howard-storm-after-he-died

Morse M with Perry P (1994) *Parting Visions* Piatkus Books, UK

Morse M with Perry P (1992) *Transformed by the Light* Piatkus Books, UK

NDE Research Foundation (2013) http://www.nderf.org/NDERF/NDE_Experiences/frank_g_fde.htm

O'Brian B (2014) *Hungry Ghosts* http://buddhism.about.com/od/buddhismglossaryh/g/hungryghostdef.htm

Pym J (2011) *Buddha and God* http://www.buddhist-christian.org/articles/0704jp.html

Ring K (1984) *Heading Toward Omega* Harper Collins, New York

Ring K and Cooper S (1999) *Mindsight* William James, New York

Rodonia G (2013) *Reverend George Rodonaia's NDE* http://www.near-death.com/experiences/evidence10.html

Sabom M (1982) *Recollections of Death* Harper and Row, New York

Sanders F (2010) *Thomas Aquinas' Big Pile of Straw* http://www.patheos.com/blogs/scriptorium/2010/12/thomas-aquinas-big-pile-of-straw/

Slick M (2014) *Purgatory* http://carm.org/purgatory

Smolowe A (2013) *Great Thoughts Treasury* http://www.greatthoughtstreasury.com/author/tripitaka-or-tipitaka?page=4

Sprigge T L S cited in Handerich T (ed) (1995) *The Philosophers* Oxford University Press, UK

Wansrough H (ed) (1990) *The New Jerusalem Bible* Darton, Longman and Todd, UK

Wilson I (1997) *Life After Death: The Evidence* Pan Books, UK

ValkyrieKerry Kelly © 2018 KM Media

Printed in Great Britain
by Amazon